Formative A̶s̶... n

K̶... 2

⌐

matched to the
National Curriculum Programme of Study
and Scheme of Work

TEACHER'S
MANUAL

Hodder & Stoughton

A MEMBER OF THE HODDER HEADLINE GROUP

*'For assessment to be formative,
the feedback information has to be used.'*

Paul Black & Dylan Wiliam, *Inside the Black Box:
Raising Standards through Classroom Assessment, 1998*

This Teacher's Manual was prepared by
Colin McCarty of GOAL plc and
Charles Knight of Hodder & Stoughton Educational

Acknowledgements
GOAL plc and Hodder & Stoughton are indebted to the teachers and their
pupils who took part in pre-testing questions

Orders: please contact Bookpoint Ltd, 130 Milton Park, Abingdon, Oxon OX14 4SB. Telephone: (44) 01235 827720, Fax: (44) 01235 400454. Lines are open from 9.00 to 6.00, Monday to Saturday, with a 24-hour message answering service. Email address: orders@bookpoint.co.uk

British Library Cataloguing in Publication Data
A catalogue record for this title is available from The British Library

ISBN 0 340 84552 X

First published 2002
Impression number   10 9 8 7 6 5 4 3 2 1
Year   2007 2006 2005 2004 2003 2002

Typeset by Dorchester Typesetting Group Ltd.
Printed in Great Britain for Hodder & Stoughton Educational, a division of Hodder Headline Plc, 338 Euston Road, London NW1 3BH, by Hobbs the Printers Ltd, Totton, Hampshire SO40 3WX.

Contents

What is GOAL Formative Assessment?

Global Online Assessment for Learning, **GOAL** plc, came into being in January 2000. The **GOAL** concept is to contribute to school improvement through data richness. As one part of this **GOAL** provides, primarily through the Internet, a variety of assessments, multiple-choice tests and diagnostic feedback for teachers and pupils. Pupils take the **GOAL** tests, which are marked and analysed and a set of useful information is sent to the school within minutes over the Internet.

The questions making up **GOAL *Formative Assessment*** were originally written for the online delivery of the **GOAL** tests, and the tests were designed to help provide the diagnostic information that allows teachers to turn summative assessment into formative assessment. **GOAL** believes that teachers have been seeking this type of help from the assessment system for many years. Nevertheless, not all schools are able to use online systems easily or with confidence. The pencil-and-paper versions are therefore designed to give teachers in these schools some of the same assessment opportunities and feedback as those who are using **GOAL** online.

The multiple-choice design of this test makes for both ease of marking and high reliability, because the scoring involves no subjectivity and maximises the opportunity for diagnostic feedback. **GOAL *Formative Assessment*** provides you with tests that give diagnostic information focused both on curriculum areas and skills for learning. It enables you to implement effective formative assessment – to manage and plan your teaching *for* learning. This is assessment that helps directly to inform and target individual and class learning strategies. It provides a simple and easy way to focus on gaps in knowledge, areas of misunderstanding and the skills being required, as well as recognising all gains in learning by your pupils. As such, formative assessment is far more useful than summative assessment in supporting you the teacher as the manager of your pupils' learning outcomes.

The tests build on all of the data gathered from online usage, backed up by a comprehensive trial involving nearly 4000 pupils, which allowed the data to be standardised and was conducted by researchers from Exeter University as well as the **GOAL** research team. These data underpin the tables and charts that enable you to make comparisons with two large cohorts of pupils. The first cohort provides the data to link the marks in this test to National Curriculum levels of attainment (page 11) and provides standardised score information (page 23). The second cohort shows the patterns of performance of pupils at different National Curriculum levels, indicating questions and areas of the curriculum that all pupils appear to find difficult or easy (page 17). These data also support diagnostic analysis of the broader skills – knowledge and understanding, using and applying, and problem-solving – which are needed to be able to answer each of the questions (page 20).

Scores obtained from the test are both reliable and valid measures of National Curriculum performance, because every question has been taken by many hundreds of pupils and their average performance has been equated to National Curriculum levels. The aggregated results obtained from the online system also give a picture of performance of each year group, against which you can compare the performance of your own pupils (page 19).

GOAL *Formative Assessment in Key Stage 2 ICT* is one of a suite of four tests at Key Stage 2, each covering levels 1–5: the other three are Literacy, Mathematics and Science. Each of these tests is designed in the same way as the ICT test, and together they may be used to compare pupils' progress across the four subjects.

GOAL *Formative Assessment* gives both summative and formative information.

For example:

- *if you need to have an external baseline for your value-added requirements, then **GOAL** tests will supply it;*
- *if you want to follow the progress of your pupils from year to year, **GOAL** tests provide you with the ideal solution;*
- *if you need to establish a National Curriculum level for each pupil, **GOAL** tests are calibrated to indicate National Curriculum levels, and they are further subdivided into upper, middle and lower – a, b and c – to provide a finer level of information;*
- *if you wish to investigate some of the strengths and weaknesses of your pupils' cognitive skills, **GOAL** tests allow this.*

Also, because it has a diagnostic, formative capability, **GOAL *Formative Assessment*** enables you to answer parents, governors, inspectors or headteachers who ask:

- *How has my child done compared to others of his or her age or year group?*
- *What sort of pattern of performance do pupils at a particular National Curriculum level achieve?*
- *What is a reasonable level of achievement for this pupil?*
- *Can you plot a pupil's progress from year to year?*
- *What are the strengths or successes of this pupil, or the class?*
- *How can pupils learn from their mistakes?*
- *On what aspects of the subject should the pupils concentrate to make sure they achieve the highest standard?*
- *Is the topic something that other teachers appear to find difficult to teach too?*

The information in this Teacher's Manual unlocks a wealth of diagnostic information that will enable you to be more effective in the management of learning in your classroom.

By using the **GOAL** record sheets provided, you can build a picture of each pupil's performances that will let you follow progress, measure value-added and provide a set of validated data for future years. The pattern revealed will in turn inform the target-setting process. Equally it will highlight the learning and cognitive skills in which pupils are confident and those that need addressing.

GOAL *Formative Assessment in Key Stage 2 ICT* comprises 50 questions, covering levels 1–5, and will take pupils up to one hour to complete if all the questions are attempted (in practice, however, this is rarely necessary – see page 15). The test has been carefully structured so that there are five sections, each of ten questions and with each section assessing one level of the National Curriculum programme of study. The test starts with ten questions at level 1, and the final ten questions are at level 5. This wide range allows use of the test with all ability groups – including the least able – across Key Stage 2, and allows all pupils to experience some success.

The test writers were given the brief to provide a wide, thorough coverage of the specific elements at each level within the National Curriculum. This has been assured by systematically sampling all key aspects of the Attainment Target in the National Curriculum for ICT, at each level, across ten curriculum strands, as shown in Table 1. It has not been possible to categorise the questions by the sub-sections of the AT, as the Attainment Target is holistic and the changing emphasis at different levels of demand in the National Curriculum has proven to make it impossible to maintain consistency within the **GOAL** curriculum strands and match them to the five sub-sections (IT1–5) of the Attainment Target. Equally, by using multiple-choice questions, which ensure a broad coverage of the programme of study, it becomes impossible to ask pupils to create, find or alter data, text or images on screen, which is also a significant element of the programme of study. Our approach, therefore, has been to define three sub-divisions of the Attainment Target – IT A, IT B and IT C – in a way which makes for coherent groupings of the curriculum strands and which allows some stability across the levels.

Sub-division of ICT Attainment Target	Sub-section of ICT Programme of Study	Curriculum strand
IT A	Use of hardware	1
	Processing and interpreting data	2
	Data retrieval	3
IT B	Use of control	4
	Use of draw, graphics and DTP	5
IT C	Searching and organising data	6
	Data base skills	7
	Internet skills	8
	Spreadsheet skills	9
	ICT in society	10

Table 1 Balance of curriculum strands

At each level, the balance of the ten questions for

IT A : IT B : IT C is **3 : 2 : 5.**

This means that elements of reviewing, modifying and evaluating work as it progresses, together with the breadth of study, are assessed by questions that also address:

- *finding things out;*
- *developing ideas and making things happen;*
- *exchanging and sharing information.*

The photocopiable Pupil Performance Profiles (page 19) enable you to focus on these three sub-divisions of the Attainment Target, as this gives you the most critical analysis in a broad-brush stroke, illustrating any aspect where pupils are under-performing.

To investigate performance at a more detailed level, note that strand 1 comprises questions 1, 11, 21, 31, etc; strand 2 is always questions 2, 12, 22, 32, etc; and so on within each block of ten questions. The Class Record Sheet (included with the packs of Test Booklets) will enable you to pick out any particular strand where a pupil is showing consistently poor performance, and this gives you the opportunity to revisit that element of the subject. It will also highlight individual strengths.

A sub-division of ICT into rigorously different areas of content or skill is impossible, particularly as the skills and use alter as pupils grow in experience. The first three **GOAL** strands are very loosely drawn from **Finding things out**, and correspond to all the sections in IT1 together with some IT4 and IT5 material set in an appropriate context. **GOAL** strands 4 and 5 loosely correspond to the sections of **Developing ideas and making things happen**, together with some IT4 and IT5 material. **GOAL** strands 6, 7, 8, 9 and 10 cover work in **Exchanging and sharing information**, again including material from IT4 and IT5.

Table 4, on page 17, shows how the questions have been classified into the skills of knowledge and understanding, using and applying, and problem-solving using Bloom's Taxonomy. This is discussed in more detail on page 20. The Class Record Sheet also enables you to investigate the skills pupils are using to answer the questions in the test, and to compare them to the external sample of over 40,000 pupils, using the photocopiable Pupil Skills Profiles (page 21).

1.   Measuring progress

The wide coverage of National Curriculum levels will enable you to use the test as an indicator to obtain a measure of progress made by your pupils and of 'value-added'. At its simplest, pupils can be asked to attempt the complete test every year, usually toward the end of the school year. The result obtained will enable you to report the year-on-year progress as:

- *a raw score out of 50;*
- *a National Curriculum level;*
- *a more finely differentiated National Curriculum level – a, b or c – where:*

    a   is fully secure at the level

    b   is comfortably at the level and

    c   indicates performance just at the level;

- *an age-standardised score;*
- *a percentile;*
- *a learning skills profile;*
- *a progress by curriculum strand (IT A, IT B, IT C) profile.*

The test may also be used in a diagnostic and formative manner, when it should be used at the *beginning* of each academic year to indicate strengths and weaknesses, to check to see if there has been any fall-back since the end of the previous year, and to provide information which will enable your lesson planning and target setting to be fully informed.

2.   National Curriculum levels and sub-levels

Table 2, on page 11, enables you to convert raw scores into National Curriculum levels, and to subdivide each level into a, b and c, as indicated above. These divisions are known as *tertiles* and are linked to the upper, middle and lower thirds of the populations in the mark range. This subdivision allows for more informative reporting to parents and pupils, and shows progress in finer increments than whole levels. It is a more volatile reporting system, however, and progress from year to year is not likely to be in steady increments.

Although age-standardised scores and percentiles can also be used to report progress, a disadvantage is that these may imply a spurious degree of precision and lead to an inappropriate emphasis on rank order. The alternative approach here, using a–c as 'bands' of achievement, is probably fairer and gives more information than levels alone, and does not give undue emphasis to small differences in scores in the same manner that an age-related rank order may.

GOAL Formative Assessment has been designed so that you can make good summative use of the test results by reviewing each pupil's performance in terms of **the degree of success at each level**. A very good rule of thumb to establish whether a pupil is secure in a given level is to require about two-thirds of the answers to be correct on questions targeted at that level. To feel confident in this judgement, you may expect that besides a significant number of marks being achieved within the level, you would expect to find the pupil gaining some marks from questions on the next higher level. Equally, total perfection on the level below is not expected, although the vast majority of the questions should be answered correctly. The following examples should help to illustrate this point.

Typical patterns for pupils at different stages in level 3 would be close to:

Level 2 9 marks   ▪ **Level 3** 6 marks   ▪ **Level 4** 2 marks

Such a pupil is confident but not wholly secure in level 3. This would probably be assessed as 3b.

The pattern below suggests that the pupil is fully secure in level 3, and is assessed as 3a:

Level 2 10 marks   ▪ **Level 3** 8 marks   ▪ **Level 4** 3 marks

A pupil who is just reaching the level 3 borderline – i.e. assessed as 3c – may show a profile similar to the one below:

Level 2 7 marks   ▪ **Level 3** 5 marks   ▪ **Level 4** 1 mark

Teachers wishing to analyse their pupils' performances in this way need to keep the scores for each group of ten questions (i.e. each level) separately in their records. The Class Record Sheet is designed to enable you to access the data quite easily.

In the **GOAL** assessments, the overall mark each pupil achieves is related to an indicative National Curriculum sub-level through a sophisticated statistical comparison using an 'Item Response Theory' (IRT) analysis package (see page 24).

IRT analysis helps to show which questions are the most difficult and which are the easiest. Table 2 gives the mark range which equates to each National Curriculum sub-level.

Range of test marks	Indicative National Curriculum sub-levels
5–6	1c
7–8	1b
9–10	1a
11–13	2c
14–16	2b
17–19	2a
20–25	3c
26–29	3b
30–32	3a
33–35	4c
36–37	4b
38–40	4a
41–42	5c
43–44	5b
45–50	5a

Table 2 Test mark ranges and indicative National Curriculum sub-levels (derived from mathematics National Curriculum levels)

3. Diagnosing strengths and weaknesses by curriculum strand

Every pupil has particular strengths and weaknesses that will show up in the test. When you examine the pupil's answers, you can check to see when there is a change from correct answers to incorrect answers, and at what level of demand this is occurring. If the pattern is fairly similar across all the curriculum strands, then the pupil is making balanced progress across the subject. If some strands show marked differences, however, this will alert you to significant extra achievement or where there is an area of the subject to be revisited. Equally, if the pattern is very patchy, you may wish to ask the pupil if there are parts of the subject, perhaps taught in earlier years, which have been forgotten or have failed to be understood at the time.

It should be borne in mind when undertaking this form of analysis that performance will naturally reflect recent teaching.

It is inappropriate solely to consider the raw scores, as this presupposes that the questions within a level are all of equal difficulty. This is patently unlikely to be so. It is therefore important to be able to compare the performance of your pupils against a large group of other pupils, to see if certain strands are more difficult than others or if the questions in one strand are more challenging compared to those in other strands. The evidence from this analysis will enable you to report substantiated data by curriculum strand for each pupil and for the class as a whole.

The (photocopiable) Pupil Performance Profiles on page 19 illustrate the average scores obtained from the complete cohort of 43,000 pupils who sat these questions in online **GOAL** tests between January and July 2001. The tinted part of each chart shows the average score in each strand for pupils at each level, enabling you to compare the performance of your own individual pupils – or, better still, the averaged performance of your class (the Class Record Sheet is designed to enable you to calculate this quite easily). By comparing your own pupil data with an externally derived set of data, you can, with confidence, decide whether the class you are teaching is doing better or less well when compared to other schools.

These data are most helpful when exploring value-added, for it remains unfair on schools to be judged as poor if they have a very weak intake. This comparison exercise enables the teacher to illustrate with confidence where the class or individual sits with respect to many other pupils from across the country and from a complete range of schools.

4. Diagnosing strengths and weaknesses by skill area

Every question in the test has been analysed for the broader skills or competences that it assesses. The details of these skills, derived from Bloom's Taxonomy, are shown in Table 5. This type of analysis is widely used by Examination Awarding Bodies to ensure that tests and examinations cover a balanced range of demands in terms of what is required from the pupil. Some subjects will obviously favour certain aspects of the skills – ICT and Science will draw upon the full range of skills, but Mathematics, for example, will focus strongly on calculation and problem-solving. The skill of evaluation is often met in English, as is analysis.

The questions in this ICT test have been classified into one of three categories:

- Knowledge & understanding   KU
- Using & applying   UA
- Problem-solving   PS

Problem-solving is deemed the highest order of the three skills and as such subsumes the other two skills. This is a fine distinction, as use and application also require the pupil to use higher-order cognitive skills. In the Class Record and Skills Profile sheets that you use to analyse and compare your pupils' performances, only the highest-order skill is shown for each question.

As with analysing curriculum strengths and weaknesses, using the Pupil Performance Profiles, it is always wise to compare the skills patterns you obtain for your own pupils with those of the external reference group of pupils. The Pupil Skills Profiles (see photocopy master on page 21) will enable you to make more refined judgments as to whether the perceived strengths and weaknesses are a feature of the group you are teaching or perhaps more widely symptomatic of pupils at this age range or level of performance.

In using skills analysis, it is important to look only for the broader patterns. There are two reasons for this. First, the nature of allocating a question to a particular skill involves human judgement, and as such will be subject to the bias of those involved in making and confirming that judgement – what is problem-solving for one person may be deemed to be application by another. Second, a higher-order skill may not necessarily be harder to display. For example, simple recall is often given as the easiest skill – but if you cannot remember a fact, it is incredibly difficult if not impossible to answer; in contrast, a problem-solving exercise often has some elements of data with which even someone who is very unsure of what they are doing may grope toward an answer.

5. Summative assessment: age-standardised scores and percentiles

Not withstanding the cautionary notes mentioned earlier, about what may be perceived as the spurious precision of age-related norms, there are a number of advantages of using age-standardised scores for comparing summative performance.

These include:

- They are standardised to an average score of 100, immediately showing whether a pupil is above or below average, compared to the reference sample.

- They allow comparisons to take into account the pupils' ages, to the nearest 3 months: older pupils are likely to have higher *raw* scores than younger pupils, but could have a lower *standardised* score. This allows pupils to be put in rank order of achievement after age has been accounted for.

- They allow a pupil's scores from different tests and in different subjects – ICT, Science, Mathematics and Literacy, in the **GOAL** suite – to be compared on a more level playing field than just using raw scores.

The danger is that age-standardised scores often give too fine a distinction – suggesting one pupil is better than another, where the confidence limit of the mark does not allow this. For this reason, performance *bands* are usually seen as fairer. However, the same issue holds true here, as one mark is all it takes to move a pupil from one band to the next. Care is therefore advised and caution should be taken when placing pupils in order of merit. The 90% confidence band for the **GOAL** assessment is plus or minus 6, so for a pupil with an age-standardised score of 106 you can be 90% confident that their 'true' score is between 100 and 112.

For teachers wishing to use age-standardised scores, therefore, Table 6, on page 23, allows you to derive both standardised scores and percentiles from pupils' raw scores, by three-monthly age ranges from 7 years to 11 years. This form of presentation helps to minimise inappropriate interpretations based on the use of age-related norms, particularly those showing differences by month.

GOAL *Formative Assessment at Key Stage 2* is designed so that the pupils answer the test in the question booklets. The answers are marked and the details transferred onto the specially designed Class Record Sheet, which may be used to investigate the performance of pupils.

The Test Booklets are designed for whole-class use, with pupils of all abilities, and the Key Stage 2 tests assess across levels 1 to 5. Given this wide coverage, it would be exceptional to require pupils to attempt all fifty questions in the test on any one occasion, and in most circumstances it is preferable (and quicker) to 'target' the test for use with each Year group as suggested below.

It is highly unlikely that Year 3 or many Year 4 pupils will have met work at level 5 and they are unlikely therefore to progress further than question 40 (i.e. covering levels 1, 2, 3 and 4). In fact, at Year 3 you may prefer only to use the first 30 questions, covering levels 1, 2 and 3, to prevent pupils from meeting questions on work that has yet to be covered. In this case, tell them not to attempt any of the higher questions, as only by chance are they likely to get any correct.

By Year 5 some pupils may be working at level 5, and all should regularly be meeting work at level 4. Depending upon the ability of the pupils, it may be more appropriate that they omit the first ten questions, which are targeted at level 1, and just take questions 11 to 50, covering levels 2–5. This is one possible strategy. Equally, some pupils may be more motivated if they find the initial questions relatively easy, so you may prefer to use these first questions for this reason.

If you do allow your pupils to omit the first ten questions and start at question 11, you should assume that they would get all the level 1 questions correct and **add ten marks** to their scores from questions 11 to 50. A similar pattern would then apply for pupils in Year 6, where they should all do questions 11 to 50, covering levels 2–5. If they start at question 11, then these pupils should be **credited with ten marks** in addition to those gained from the forty questions actually taken.

Table 3 illustrates these ways of using the test in each year and awarding the marks. Irrespective of how the test is taken, it is recommended that you always record the test score as being out of 50 so that an increasing score will show the value added across Key Stage 2. The test is not 'speeded', and most pupils will complete it quite comfortably within the maximum time suggested in the table.

Year	Question range	Question levels	Maximum time to allow for test	Add to score to get mark from a total of 50
3	1–30	1–3	20 mins	0
4	1–40	1–4	30 mins	0
5	11–50	2–5	30 mins	10
6	11–50	2–5	30 mins	10

Table 3 Suggested test ranges for different years

Recording results: the Class Record Sheet

1 Mark the Test Booklets against the answers given in Table 4, using the mark boxes on the right-hand side of each page in the Test Booklet.

2 Add the ticks in the mark boxes to get each pupil's total score and complete the Totals column on the Class Record Sheet. (Remember to include full marks for lower levels which the pupil was told not to take.)

3 Use Table 6 on page 23 of this manual to enter the pupil's standardised score and percentile, in the columns headed SS and %.

4 To get fuller information about performance at each level, count the correct answers for the first ten questions and write this in the level 1 column on the Class Record Sheet. Now repeat for questions 11 to 20 and place this total in the level 2 column. Continue for levels 3, 4 and 5.

5 To find the total for IT A, inspect the mark boxes and count the ticks in those boxes which have 'IT A' written *above* them. Transfer this total to the Class Record Sheet. Repeat for IT B and IT C.

6 Similarly, for the Skills profile, count and record the number of correct answers categorised *below* each mark box as KU (knowledge & understanding), UA (using & applying) and PS (problem-solving).

7 For each curriculum strand, and skill area, if required, you can then work out average scores for your class. These will enable you to compare your class to an external sample of pupils, or find if individual pupils are stronger or weaker relative to their class or to an external sample of pupils from the same year, using either or both of the Pupil Performance and Skills Profiles.

For convenience, information about what is being tested and pupils' performance on the questions is brought together in Table 4. This shows, for every question, the correct answer and the skill being tested. It also shows, for each question, the percentage success, or facility, for pupils who were judged to be operating at each level. These data were obtained from the **GOAL** online server and collected from all the tests taken between January and July 2001.

Question number	Correct answer	Bloom skill	AT Sub-division	NC level	Facility*	Question number	Correct answer	Bloom skill	AT Sub-division	NC level	Facility*
1	D	UA	IT A	1	87	26	A	KU	IT C	3	76
2	A	KU	IT A	1	72	27	B	UA	IT C	3	72
3	D	KU	IT A	1	67	28	D	KU	IT C	3	75
4	D	KU	IT B	1	59	29	B	UA	IT C	3	81
5	B	KU	IT B	1	81	30	A	KU	IT C	3	82
6	B	UA	IT C	1	75	31	A	KU	IT A	4	82
7	C	PS	IT C	1	81	32	D	KU	IT A	4	87
8	B	KU	IT C	1	75	33	A	UA	IT A	4	30
9	D	UA	IT C	1	64	34	B	PS	IT B	4	40
10	C	UA	IT C	1	75	35	D	UA	IT B	4	78
11	D	KU	IT A	2	57	36	C	PS	IT C	4	51
12	B	KU	IT A	2	58	37	C	KU	IT C	4	68
13	D	UA	IT A	2	31	38	A	KU	IT C	4	36
14	B	PS	IT B	2	81	39	C	PS	IT C	4	51
15	C	UA	IT B	2	77	40	B	KU	IT C	4	64
16	C	PS	IT C	2	86	41	A	KU	IT A	5	83
17	B	KU	IT C	2	84	42	C	UA	IT A	5	87
18	A	UA	IT C	2	84	43	A	KU	IT A	5	72
19	C	KU	IT C	2	78	44	A	PS	IT B	5	72
20	C	KU	IT C	2	81	45	C	UA	IT B	5	30
21	A	KU	IT A	3	85	46	C	PS	IT C	5	52
22	B	KU	IT A	3	63	47	B	UA	IT C	5	63
23	A	UA	IT A	3	80	48	B	KU	IT C	5	88
24	C	PS	IT B	3	76	49	C	PS	IT C	5	47
25	A	UA	IT B	3	70	50	C	KU	IT C	5	50

* The *facility* shows the percentage of successful answers given by pupils who achieved that level in the tests overall. For example, in question 26 the facility of 76% indicates that 76% of pupils who achieved level 3 got this question correct.

Table 4 Mark scheme

Recording and interpreting pupil progress

The shaded parts of the Pupil Performance Profiles (page 19) are based on the performance of the pupils who took online **GOAL** tests between January and July 2001. By reference to the patterns established by different cohorts of pupils, you can see how pupils in a particular Year have performed. A comparison of the performance profile for individual pupils – and if you are able to collate the information together, your class – will enable you to make judgements as to any areas in which your pupils are doing better than others or where they may be falling behind.

For example, if yours is a Year 5 class or teaching group, you should use the profile of performance of Year 5 pupils to compare the way each of your pupils did against the external sample of pupils. (You can compare your class averages for the three curriculum strands in the same way.) The example below shows the performance of a pupil in Year 5 and how he compares to the external sample. Scoring 29 overall, in IT C he was significantly better than the external sample, but was below average performance in IT A, and on the average in IT B.

Curriculum strand	Score achieved in each AT strand For comparison the sample performance is shown as a shaded bar chart
	1 2 3 4 5 6 7 8 9 10 11 12 13 14 15 16 17 18 19 20 21 22 23 24 25
IT A	
IT B	
IT C	

Year 5 Pupil profile of performance

The photocopiable Pupil Performance Profile has been designed so that it can become the year-on-year record of pupil progress as they move up the school. To complete your own Pupil Performance Profiles, take each pupil's raw score on each curriculum strand in turn, and mark a short vertical line to indicate the number of the questions the pupil has answered correctly. The line charts for each strand, and how each relates to the external sample, will begin to emerge.

The external comparisons provided by the tinted areas are extremely valuable, as they enable you to see at a glance whether the pupils – or class, if you average the results – are above, below or about the national average. It is particularly helpful to use this indicator of progress as pupils move from one Year to the next, to spot if there is any surge in performance or fall back. (There is also space on the Profile to record a pupil's indicative National Curriculum level, standardised score and/or percentile, if you wish.)

The Profiles may also be helpful to use with parents to provide externally validated objectivity to your discussions.

GOAL Formative Assessment in Key Stage 2 ICT: Pupil Performance Profile

Name of Pupil _____

Year 3   **Date** _____

Curriculum strand	Score achieved in each strand For comparison the sample performance is shown as a shaded bar chart
	1 2 3 4 5 6 7 8 9 10 11 12 13 14 15 16 17 18 19 20 21 22 23 24 25

IT A

IT B

IT C

Indicative NC level _____ SS _____ Percentile _____

Year 4   **Date** _____

Curriculum strand	Score achieved in each strand For comparison the sample performance is shown as a shaded bar chart
	1 2 3 4 5 6 7 8 9 10 11 12 13 14 15 16 17 18 19 20 21 22 23 24 25

IT A

IT B

IT C

Indicative NC level _____ SS _____ Percentile _____

Year 5   **Date** _____

Curriculum strand	Score achieved in each strand For comparison the sample performance is shown as a shaded bar chart
	1 2 3 4 5 6 7 8 9 10 11 12 13 14 15 16 17 18 19 20 21 22 23 24 25

IT A

IT B

IT C

Indicative NC level _____ SS _____ Percentile _____

Year 6   **Date** _____

Curriculum strand	Score achieved in each strand For comparison the sample performance is shown as a shaded bar chart
	1 2 3 4 5 6 7 8 9 10 11 12 13 14 15 16 17 18 19 20 21 22 23 24 25

IT A

IT B

IT C

Indicative NC level _____ SS _____ Percentile _____

Skills analysis

As described on page 13, the ICT questions have been classified as assessing knowledge & understanding (KU), using & applying (UA) or problem-solving (PS). Table 5 shows more details about the skills categories. These categories are shown in the Test Booklet below the mark box for each question.

To find each pupil's totals for the three skills, count the number of correct answers for each category, KU, UA and PS, and transfer each total to the corresponding column on the Class Record Sheet. Plot these, for each pupil, on the Pupil Skills Profile (see page 21) – as on the Pupil Performance Profile, the tints indicate where individual pupils are stronger or weaker relative to the external sample of pupils from the same Year.

Class averages may also be worked out and plotted on the Profile and these also compared, so that future teaching may focus on any serious weaknesses, which then may be addressed and rectified.

Competence	Skills Demonstrated
Knowledge & understanding	■ Observation and recall of information ■ Knowledge and technical terms ■ Knowledge of major ideas and subject matter ■ Understand information ■ Translate knowledge into new context ■ Interpret facts ■ Order, group, infer causes ■ Identification of components *Question Cues:* List, define, describe, identify, show, label, collect, tabulate, name, which, what, when, where, how
Using & applying	■ Use information to obtain an answer ■ Use knowledge and skill to reach a conclusion ■ Select appropriate examples ■ Use information to obtain an answer ■ Use relationships to determine amounts ■ Seeing patterns and organisation of parts *Question Cues:* Apply, demonstrate, complete, illustrate, show, connect, classify, arrange, divide, select, explain, work out
Problem-solving	■ Use methods, concepts, theories in new situations ■ Solve problems using required skills or knowledge ■ Compare and discriminate ■ Assess and verify values ■ Make choices based on reasoned argument *Question Cues:* Modify, examine, relate, change, assess, decide, rank, measure, calculate, recommend, judge, conclude, solve, compare, contrast, summarise

Table 5 ICT Skills, adapted from Bloom's Taxonomy

GOAL Formative Assessment in Key Stage 2 ICT: *Pupil Skills Profile*

Name

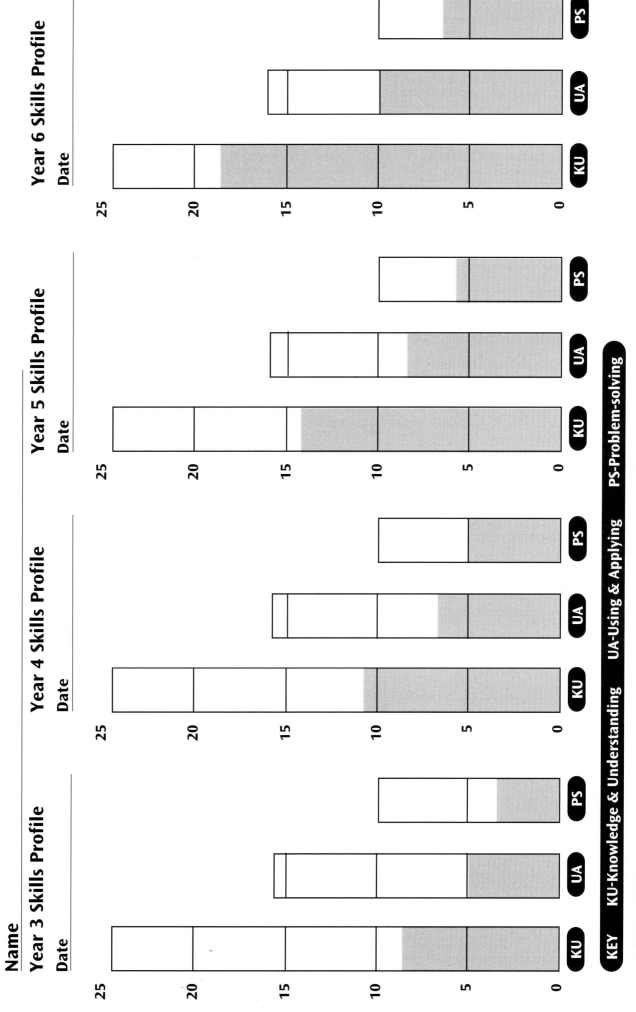

Standardised scores and percentiles

To obtain age-standardised scores, refer to Table 6. Look down the appropriate age column for the pupil and find the row containing the range of marks in which their own raw score belongs. The percentile is shown in the left-hand column and the standardised score in the right-hand column. Pupils in the 90th–99th percentile row are in the top 10% of all pupils taking the test. 'Average' pupils are in the 50th–59th row, with an age-standardised score of 100.

Standardised scores and percentiles are provided from age 7 years to 10 years 11 months: the small numbers of eleven-year-old pupils taking the test in Year 6 did not support the provision of reliable data for older pupils. Given that formative assessment is intended principally to inform ongoing teaching, and hence will be of most value *before* the end of the school year, however, this is unlikely to be a problem in practice.

It should be remembered when using this table that a 90% confidence band would indicate that all the pupils with an age-standardised score of between 96 and 104 are on a par with each other: if they took the test again, there is a 90% chance that their mark would fall in this range.

Percentile ranges	7 years				8 years				9 years				10 years				Standardised scores
	0–2	3–5	6–8	9–11	0–2	3–5	6–8	9–11	0–2	3–5	6–8	9–11	0–2	3–5	6–8	9–11	
90–99	29+	29+	30+	31+	31+	32+	33+	34+	36+	37+	39+	41+	44+	44+	45+	46+	119+
80–89	26–28	27–28	28–29	28–30	28–30	29–31	30–32	31–33	33–35	34–36	34–38	35–40	42–43	43–43	43–44	45–45	113
70–79	23–25	24–26	25–27	26–27	26–27	27–28	27–29	28–30	29–32	30–33	31–33	31–34	38–41	40–42	42–42	43–44	108
60–69	19–22	20–23	21–24	22–25	22–25	23–26	24–26	24–27	26–28	27–29	28–30	28–30	32–37	33–39	35–41	37–42	104
50–59	17–18	18–19	19–20	19–21	20–21	20–22	21–23	21–23	23–25	24–26	25–27	25–27	28–31	30–32	32–34	32–36	100
40–49	14–16	15–17	17–18	17–18	17–19	18–19	19–20	19–20	21–22	22–23	22–24	23–24	22–27	25–29	25–31	27–31	96
30–39	12–13	12–14	14–16	15–16	15–16	15–17	15–18	16–18	17–20	18–21	19–21	20–22	20–21	20–24	23–24	25–26	92
20–29	10–11	10–11	12–13	13–14	13–14	13–14	13–14	13–15	15–16	16–17	17–18	18–19	17–19	17–19	20–22	22–24	87
10–19	7–9	9–9	10–11	10–12	10–12	10–12	11–12	11–12	12–14	13–15	14–16	14–17	14–16	15–16	17–19	17–21	81
0–9	<7	<9	<10	<10	<10	<10	<11	<11	<12	<13	<14	<14	<14	<15	<16	<16	<80

Age in years and months

Table 6 Standardised scores and percentiles, for ages in three-month cohorts

Development and Standardisation

In April 2001, some 1000 pupils in 20 primary and almost 3000 pupils in 12 secondary schools, selected to form a wide demographic and geographic sample across England, took part in a trialling and equating exercise of **GOAL** tests. An analysis of the schools by Key Stage 2 and Key Stage 3 'league tables' for 2000 indicates that the samples were likely to contain the full range of pupils for each key stage in a similar proportion to the national picture.

School	Rural	Urban	Inner city	Pupils
Primary	8	10	2	967
Secondary	2	7	3	2714

Table 7 The pre-test sample

The pupils sat tests in Mathematics, Literacy, Science and ICT. These tests were built of two parts: new questions being trialled and linked to the National Curriculum standards, and special anchor questions which enable the researchers to link the standards from one test with the standards from other tests that also include these anchor questions. The trials were designed to obtain a secure correlation between performance of pupils on the anchor questions and the performance of these same pupils in the English National Curriculum tests they took in May 2001.

Between January and July 2001 almost 43,000 pupils sat the **GOAL** tests online, including the anchor questions. This sample of results has enabled the researchers at Exeter University and **GOAL** to undertake the correlation between the National Curriculum standards and the **GOAL** Formative Assessment.

The anchor questions act like a set of pegs on a scale going from easy to hard, against which the performance of other questions can be placed. The methodology used to undertake this process is called Item Response Theory or IRT. There were two anchor questions at every level in the tests used in the trials. These questions were also present in the online tests. Across the fifty questions in this test there are ten questions which act as locating points to link standards.